BUILDING BY DESIGN

ENGINEERING
THE TAJ MAHAL

BY LAURA K. MURRAY

CONTENT CONSULTANT
Stuart Tappin
Stand Consulting Engineers, London

Cover image: The Taj Mahal towers over the tourists who come to see its world-famous architecture.

Core Library

An Imprint of Abdo Publishing
abdopublishing.com

abdopublishing.com

Published by Abdo Publishing, a division of ABDO, PO Box 398166, Minneapolis, Minnesota 55439. Copyright © 2018 by Abdo Consulting Group, Inc. International copyrights reserved in all countries. No part of this book may be reproduced in any form without written permission from the publisher. Core Library™ is a trademark and logo of Abdo Publishing.

Printed in the United States of America, North Mankato, Minnesota
082017
012018

THIS BOOK CONTAINS RECYCLED MATERIALS

Cover Photo: Shutterstock Images
Interior Photos: Shutterstock Images, 1, 4–5, 19, 27, 43; Paul Prescott/Shutterstock Images, 6–7; Nicolas Economou/NurPhoto/Getty Images, 9; Red Line Editorial, 11; Payag/Metropolitan Museum of Art, 12; Jerry Irwin/Science Source, 14–15; W. Buss/DeAgostini/Getty Images, 17, 45; iStockphoto, 21; Pius Lee/Shutterstock Images, 24–25; V. S. Anandhakrishna/Shutterstock Images, 29; G. Nimatallah/DeAgostini/Getty Images, 30; Dmitry Rukhlenko/Shutterstock Images, 32–33; Pankaj Nangia/Bloomberg/Getty Images, 36–37; Universal History Archive/Universal Images Group/Getty Images, 38; Maciej Noskowski/iStockphoto, 40

Editor: Arnold Ringstad
Imprint Designer: Maggie Villaume
Series Design Direction: Laura Polzin

Publisher's Cataloging-in-Publication Data

Names: Murray, Laura K., author.
Title: Engineering the Taj Mahal / by Laura K. Murray.
Description: Minneapolis, Minnesota : Abdo Publishing, 2018. | Series: Building by design | Includes online resources and index.
Identifiers: LCCN 2017946985 | ISBN 9781532113789 (lib.bdg.) | ISBN 9781532152665 (ebook)
Subjects: LCSH: Architecture, Mogul Empire--Juvenile literature. | Buildings--Juvenile literature. | Taj Mahal (Agra, India)--Juvenile literature. | India--Agra--Juvenile literature.
Classification: DDC 726.8095--dc23
LC record available at https://lccn.loc.gov/2017946985

CONTENTS

CHAPTER ONE
A Royal Resting Place 4

CHAPTER TWO
Grand Designs. 14

CHAPTER THREE
Getting to Work 24

CHAPTER FOUR
Taking Care of the Taj Mahal 32

Fast Facts. 42

Stop and Think. 44

Glossary. 46

Online Resources 47

Learn More 47

Index 48

About the Author. 48

CHAPTER ONE

A ROYAL RESTING PLACE

It is dawn in Agra. This city is in northern India. The sun is rising. A domed building sits on the south bank of the Yamuna River. It rises from a square platform. The building is known as the Taj Mahal. It is a mausoleum. Four towers surround it. They are called minarets.

A square garden lies before the Taj Mahal. It is lined neatly with trees. Walkways divide the garden into smaller squares. A reflecting pool mirrors the towering tomb.

The sun rises behind the domes of the Taj Mahal.

The large Taj Mahal complex includes multiple buildings.

    In the dawn light, the mausoleum glows a soft pink. The color changes throughout the day as the sun moves. It shines blue, yellow, red, or bright white. Under the moon, it gleams like a jewel.

Inside the mausoleum is a queen's grave. Her name was Mumtaz Mahal. At her side is the king who built this tomb. They lie together for eternity.

THE TOMB'S NAME

Europeans first referred to Mumtaz Mahal as Taj Mahal during her tomb's construction. It means "crown of the palace." They may have picked up the term from Agra residents. At some point, people began calling her tomb the same name. The locals called the mausoleum Rauza-I Munawara when it was built. This means "the Illumined Tomb." The name refers to the way the mausoleum appears to glow. This glow occurs because the Taj Mahal is covered in white marble. The marble absorbs and reflects sunlight.

THE MAJESTIC TAJ MAHAL

The Taj Mahal is one of the world's most famous buildings. The tomb and its garden are the main parts of the overall complex. The entire complex spans 42 acres (17 ha). A mosque stands to the west of the tomb building. A guesthouse stands to the east. Both are made of red sandstone. Other elements include courtyards, galleries, and bazaar streets. Each part was included for balance.

The inside of the mosque is decorated with complex patterns.

PERSPECTIVES
INSPIRING WORDS

For centuries, people have seen the construction of the Taj Mahal as a love story. It has inspired writers, artists, and others. Rabindranath Tagore (1861–1941) was a Bengali poet. He described the Taj Mahal:

You knew, [Shah Jahan], life and youth, wealth, and glory, they all drift away in the current of time. You strove, therefore, to perpetuate only the sorrow of your heart. . . . Let the splendor of diamond, pearl, and ruby vanish like the magic shimmer of the rainbow. Only let this one tear-drop, this Tajmahal, glisten spotlessly bright on the cheek of time, forever and ever.

The Taj Mahal was constructed during the Mughal empire. The Mughals came to India from Central Asia. They were at their height of power between the 1500s and 1700s. They valued art and science.

The Taj Mahal is an example of the Mughals' royal architecture. This style has Central Asian, Indian, Persian, and European influences. The majestic mausoleum showed the empire's power and

CITIES OF
INDIA

Agra was once a capital of the Mughal Empire. Today, New Delhi is the capital of India. What do you notice about the location of Agra and other major northern cities? Why do you think Shah Jahan chose to build the Taj Mahal in Agra?

A portrait of Shah Jahan dating to the 1600s

wealth. To many people, the Taj Mahal is also a symbol of undying love.

A MONUMENT TO MUMTAZ

Shah Jahan was the fifth ruler of the Mughal empire. In 1612, he married Arjumand Banu Begum. She was not his only wife. However, she was his favorite. He gave her the name Mumtaz Mahal. This means "Chosen One of the Palace." Mumtaz died after giving birth in 1631.

Shah Jahan was heartbroken. For years, he did not listen to music or wear colorful clothing. He decided to build a grand tomb for Mumtaz. It was to be a copy of her home in the afterlife.

Building this great monument would take careful planning. It would need the finest materials. Its walls, foundations, arches, domes, and columns would require exact calculations. The emperor was aiming for perfection. His engineers were up to the task.

EXPLORE ONLINE

Chapter One discusses Shah Jahan and the Taj Mahal. Visit the website below for more information on this topic. How is the information from the website the same as the information in Chapter One? What new information did you learn from the website?

THE TAJ MAHAL
abdocorelibrary.com/engineering-taj-mahal

CHAPTER
TWO

GRAND DESIGNS

As emperor, Shah Jahan is credited as the chief architect of the Taj Mahal. He funded the project. He was also closely involved with the planning. A team of people supervised the design.

Few details are available about these architects. At the time, they were viewed merely as helpers to the emperor. Ustad Ahmad Lahauri is widely believed to have been the main architect. Mir Abd-ul Karim and Makramat Khan were construction supervisors.

The first step was finding a location. The architects based their plan on Agra's riverfront

The grand scale of the Taj Mahal was made possible by a skilled team of engineers and architects.

PERSPECTIVES
MIXING ELEMENTS

Designers mixed various styles to create the Taj Mahal. They were inspired by the Mughals' homeland. They were also inspired by Hindu and Islamic architecture. The tomb of another Mughal ruler, Humayun, influenced the Taj Mahal designers too. Like the Taj Mahal, Humayun's tomb had a grand dome. Humayun's wife, Bega Begum, had ordered the tomb built. It was completed in 1572.

gardens. But Mumtaz's monument would be built on a much grander scale. The team chose a scenic area on the Yamuna River. It would offer the perfect backdrop to the tomb.

The nearness of the river served additional purposes. It would be useful for transporting materials. The tomb would be along the waterfront rather than in the middle of the complex. This would make it visible from other riverside gardens.

The Yamuna River was a useful transportation route during the construction process.

MIRROR IMAGES

Every element in the Taj Mahal played a role in its overall balance. If a single piece were missing, the balance would be ruined. The marble mausoleum was the key feature.

Shah Jahan's architects relied on geometry in their design. Their detailed grid systems were based on a unit of measurement called a *gaz*. One *gaz* was equal to approximately 32 inches (81 cm). For the mausoleum, designers used a 7-*gaz* grid. Other buildings in the Taj Mahal complex had their own grids. The architects placed smaller grids onto an overall grid. They even had grids for building heights.

The architects used bilateral symmetry. This means one side mirrors the other. Main features, such as the mausoleum, were placed along a central axis. The axis runs north to south. Twin buildings, such as the guesthouse and the mosque, rest on either side of the central axis. Likewise, the gardens are divided

LAYOUT OF THE
TAJ MAHAL

The mausoleum is the main feature of the Taj Mahal complex. What do you notice about the buildings' positions? What do you notice about the garden? How does this help you understand the designers' plan? Why do you think math was important to this plan?

into equal sections. These are divided into further sections. A center pool also adds balance. It reflects the main mausoleum.

LEANING PILLARS

Minarets are important parts of Islamic architecture. At a mosque, a crier performs calls to prayer from them. The Taj Mahal's four minarets add balance. They help make the mausoleum look three-dimensional.

Engineers designed the minarets to lean outward. This creates an optical illusion. The minarets appear to be vertical. This effect is known as parallax. Parallax is the way an object's position seems to change if viewed from different points. The outward leaning minarets also serve as protection. Earthquakes occur in this area of India. If the minarets collapsed, they would fall away from the tomb.

HIDDEN SYMBOLS

The Taj Mahal complex has two main zones. They are symbols of the spiritual and material worlds.

The complex's lush gardens are divided into geometrically precise areas.

The northern zone relates to death. It includes the mausoleum and its buildings. The southern zone relates to life. It includes the bazaar area. These themes carry into the garden. Cypress trees are symbols of death. Fruit trees are symbols of life.

The designers arranged colors to show what was important. This is known as hierarchy. The main building was the mausoleum. It was the only all-white building. Shah Jahan considered white marble a royal material. Shapes also had a special order. They built up to the mausoleum and its central dome. For example, the bazaar area had simple columns. The mausoleum area had large columns.

POWER OF FOUR

In Islam, four is a holy number. Many patterns in the Taj Mahal are based on the number four and its multiples. Each of the tomb's four sides is identical. Four smaller domes surround its large central dome. Mumtaz's burial chamber is an octagon. Four corner rooms surround the center chamber.

The plans were laid out with careful detail. Now it was time to build. The engineers would need workers and skilled artists to carry out their grand designs.

STRAIGHT TO THE SOURCE

A man named Raja Jai Singh owned the land on which the Taj Mahal was to be built. In 1632, the empire sent royal orders to Singh. The following was one of them:

> To the best of equals and grandees, the pride of peers and contemporaries, worthy of attention and favors, the sincere, loyal, and devoted servant Raja Jai Singh.
>
> And we hereby order that, whatever the number of stone-cutters and carts-on-hire for loading the stone that may be required . . . the Raja should make them available to him; and the wages of the stone-cutters and rent-money of the carts, he will provide with funds from the royal treasurer. . . . [H]e should consider this a matter of utmost importance, and not deviate from this order.

Source: Frank P. Davidson and Kathleen Lusk Brooke. *Building the World: An Encyclopedia of the Great Engineering Projects in History*. Vol 1. Westport, CT: Greenwood, 2006. Print. 116.

Consider Your Audience

Adapt this passage as a blog post for a different audience, such as your principal or friends. How does your post differ from the original text and why?

CHAPTER THREE

GETTING TO WORK

A reported 20,000 people helped build the Taj Mahal. Many were from northern India. Some traveled from as far as Syria and Persia. Workers were sculptors, carvers, bricklayers, and stonecutters. Others were skilled in building domes or turrets.

By January 1632, workers had begun laying the mausoleum's foundations. This was the most important part of construction. It was also the most challenging. The tomb and its main buildings would rest on a terrace. The terrace's foundations would lie in the sandy riverbank. To support the terrace, workers dug

The edge of the Taj Mahal's foundation

25

PERSPECTIVES
ROYAL MATERIAL

When built, the Taj Mahal had the largest amount of white marble ever used in an Indian building. Historian Giles Tillotson writes:

> Shah Jahan consciously reserved white marble for buildings associated with himself. In the fort at Agra, he demolished some of the older sandstone palaces . . . and replaced them with his own marble ones, to project his pure heart and spiritual nature. Against this record it is hardly surprising that the same material was chosen for the Taj. But the scale was unprecedented and so, as a result, is its impact. . . . The sheer quantity of white stone that confronts us on entering the garden of the Taj is overwhelming.

deep wells. They filled the wells with iron and roughly cut stone.

Throughout the complex, workers built strong supporting walls. They filled the walls with stone or bricks in mortar. They covered the walls with slabs of red sandstone. This helped to strengthen the structures.

MATERIALS AND TECHNIQUES

Every building in the complex was made of brick. Workers

White marble is still quarried in India today.

made the bricks in kilns near Agra. White marble and sandstone came from distant quarries. Teams of animals hauled carts of the materials to Agra. Sometimes, workers used plaster as a cheaper finish. To make the plaster, they mixed ground shells, sugar, egg whites, plant fibers, and other materials. They polished the plaster so it gleamed like marble.

Stoneworkers used wedges, hammers, and saws to cut stone blocks. The builders used wooden ramps to move heavy materials. They likely used traditional scaffolding made of bamboo.

WORKING WITH STONES

Workers used valuable stones to decorate the Taj Mahal. Many came from around India. These included garnet, sapphire, onyx, and topaz. Other materials came from farther away. Jade and crystal were brought from Central Asia. Turquoise came from Tibet. Yellow amber arrived from Burma. Lapis lazuli was from Afghanistan. Workers used traditional Mughal techniques. They also used a technique they learned from Italian artists. It is called *pietra dura*. It involves using many cut stones to create images.

DOUBLE DOME

The large central dome is one of the most dramatic features of the mausoleum. It rises to a height of 240 feet (73 m). The tomb walls needed to be able to support it.

Workers built thick walls out of bricks and a type of limestone mortar. They faced the walls with marble slabs. The slabs were tied together with iron clamps. The central

Four smaller domes surround the Taj Mahal's grand central dome.

dome itself was made of two domes. The inside dome is low and rounded. The outside dome is tall and pointed. The domes keep the design balanced.

FINAL BURIAL

In 1633, Mumtaz was given a final burial. Her burial marker was placed in a two-story chamber. It is in the exact center of the building. The chamber has eight sides. The walls and marker are highly decorated. The floor has geometric patterns.

This chamber is empty. Mumtaz's body is in a private chamber below. She was placed along the north-and-south axis. Her head was turned to the west.

The tombs of Mumtaz and Shah Jahan lie within the building's interior.

This is the direction of Mecca. Mecca is the holiest city for Muslims. They face it when praying.

A FINISHED PROJECT

By 1643, the mausoleum was officially complete. The entire complex was finished ten years later. Afterward, the tomb required money for upkeep and staff. To pay for this, the Taj Mahal had a trust. It received income from 30 Agra villages. It also earned money from its shops and fruit trees.

In 1666, Shah Jahan died. His burial marker was placed next to Mumtaz's. In the room below, his grave was placed alongside his wife's.

STRAIGHT TO THE SOURCE

James Fergusson was a Scottish historian. He studied Indian architecture. In 1876, Fergusson wrote the following about the Taj Mahal:

> *If the Taj were only the tomb itself, it might be described, but the platform on which it stands, with its tall minarets, is a work of art in itself. Beyond this are the two wings, one of which is a mosque, which anywhere else would be considered an important building. . . . Beautiful as it is in itself, the Taj would lose half its charm if it stood alone. It is the combination of so many beauties, and the perfect manner in which each is subordinated to the other, that makes up a whole which the world cannot match, and which never fails to impress even those who are most indifferent to the effects produced by architectural objects in general.*

Source: Giles Tillotson. *Taj Mahal*. Cambridge, MA: Harvard University, 2008. Ebook. April 1, 2017. 96.

What's the Big Idea?

Take a close look at this passage. What is the main point being made about the Taj Mahal? What does Fergusson think about the different parts of the complex? Does this support what you know about the designers' plans? Why or why not?

CHAPTER FOUR

TAKING CARE OF THE TAJ MAHAL

Today, millions of people visit the Taj Mahal each year. The tomb has up to 45,000 visitors a day during peak season. Some Muslims and Hindus consider it a sacred site. The tomb is also a popular place for tourists.

The monument is open year-round. October through March is the busiest visiting time. Many people visit at sunrise or sunset. They enjoy the changing colors of the marble tomb.

Tourists from around the world come to India to see the Taj Mahal complex.

WEAR AND TEAR

The Taj Mahal has experienced normal wear. As early as 1652, its leaking domes needed repairs. Parts of its buildings have become discolored. Slabs sometimes crack. Still, the structure has stood through earthquakes, storms, and floods.

ANOTHER VIEW

Most images of the Taj Mahal show the tomb sitting behind its reflecting pool. This is the way visitors approach the tomb on foot. However, this side is the building's rear. The front faces the Yamuna River. Mughal rulers visited the tomb by boat. They docked their barges next to the platform. Then they followed stairs up to the mausoleum.

Pollution is a serious concern. Polluted air has turned the marble yellow and brown. In 1996, the Supreme Court of India gave orders to protect it from pollution. Factories and vehicles were banned nearby.

Today, the Indian government manages the Taj Mahal. A control station monitors the air quality

But pollution is increasing nearby. At times, the Taj Mahal has been hidden by thick smog.

NEW CHALLENGES

Tourists add to the upkeep challenges. Their footsteps wear out the paving. Sometimes tourists write on the walls. They pick at the stonework.

Another concern is commercial development. Through the years, companies have proposed tourist attractions nearby. Laws are in place to protect the Taj Mahal from development.

Other threats come from war and terrorism. In 1984,

> **PERSPECTIVES**
> ### WORLD HERITAGE SITE
> In 1983, the Taj Mahal was named a World Heritage Site by the United Nations Educational, Scientific, and Cultural Organization (UNESCO). This means the area has significance and deserves special legal protections. UNESCO said, "The Taj Mahal is the jewel of Muslim art in India and one of the universally admired masterpieces of the world's heritage."

The nearby Yamuna River is badly polluted.

militants threatened to bomb the building. In 2001, security was increased following major terrorist attacks in the United States. That same year, a giant cloth was created. It could hide the tomb in the event

of a Pakistani airstrike. The tomb had previously been covered with scaffolding during World War II (1939–1945). It was also covered during wars with Pakistan in 1965 and 1971.

CLEANING AND TREATING

Plans have been put in place to ensure the Taj Mahal's upkeep. In 2015, the government began a maintenance project. It is meant to fix the minarets' discoloration.

Occasionally, the tomb receives a surface treatment. This work helps restore the building's glow. Workers cover the marble with a brown paste. It is known as *multani mitti*. The paste is made of soil, milk, and lime. After 24 hours, they wash off the dried paste. Archaeologists say the paste draws out pollutants from the marble. Traditionally, many Indian women have used the same treatment on their skin.

Rumors and debates often arise over the tomb's condition. In 2011, activists claimed the monument could collapse soon. They said the wooden foundation was rotting. The authorities denied any danger of collapse. Some people worried about leaning minarets. Others were concerned about dropping river levels.

US troops visit the Taj Mahal in 1942. Scaffolding covers the dome behind them.

> ## FURTHER EVIDENCE
>
> Chapter Four has information about the legacy of the Taj Mahal. What was one of the main points of this chapter? What key evidence supports this point? Watch the video at the website below. Does the information on the website support the main point of this chapter? Does it present new evidence?
>
> ### UNESCO: TAJ MAHAL
> abdocorelibrary.com/engineering-taj-mahal

Most of these issues have been dismissed. However, detailed studies of the foundation are difficult. They could harm the structure.

A MONUMENT FOR THE AGES

To many in India, the Taj Mahal is a national treasure. It has been called one of the wonders of the modern world. Centuries after its construction, the mausoleum still amazes visitors. Architects, engineers, and historians alike marvel at its beauty and design. The engineering of the Taj Mahal highlights a ruler's power. It also showcases a love that lasted beyond death.

Workers apply a treatment to the surface of one of the complex's minarets.

FAST FACTS

- The Taj Mahal is a mausoleum located in Agra, India, along the Yamuna River.
- The mausoleum is the main feature of the larger Taj Mahal complex.
- The Mughal ruler Shah Jahan built the Taj Mahal for his favorite wife, Mumtaz Mahal.
- The construction of the mausoleum lasted from 1632 to 1643.
- Shah Jahan is credited as chief designer. However, a team of architects led the work.
- Every element in the Taj Mahal plays a role in the overall balance and symmetry.
- Shah Jahan's architects relied on geometry and grids in their design.
- Approximately 20,000 workers helped build the Taj Mahal.
- The Taj Mahal's buildings are made of brick. They are faced with white marble, red sandstone, and polished plaster.
- The burial markers of Mumtaz Mahal and Shah Jahan sit in the tomb's octagonal burial chamber. Their real graves lie in the room below.

- Modern threats to the tomb include deterioration, pollution, tourists, commercial development, and terrorism.

- Conservation plans have been put in place to protect and repair the structure.

STOP AND
THINK

Tell the Tale

Chapter Two discusses the planning of the Taj Mahal. Imagine you are an architect on Shah Jahan's team. Write 200 words about the experience. What types of things do you need to keep in mind while planning?

Dig Deeper

After reading this book, what questions do you still have about the upkeep of the Taj Mahal? With an adult's help, find a few reliable sources that can help you answer your questions. Then write a paragraph about what you learned.

Say What?

Studying the engineering of the Taj Mahal can mean learning new vocabulary. Find five words in this book you had never heard before. Use the glossary or a dictionary to find out what they mean. Then write the meanings in your own words. Use each word in a new sentence.

You Are There

This book discusses the materials and techniques used to build the Taj Mahal. Imagine you are in charge of the builders and artists. Write a blog post about your experience. What sorts of materials do your workers use? What tools do they have?

GLOSSARY

axis
a straight line that divides something in half

bazaar
a marketplace

commercial
for the purpose of making money

geometry
the branch of math that includes measurements, lines, angles, and shapes

hierarchy
a system of ranking in order of importance

kilns
ovens that bake or dry objects

mausoleum
a burial chamber that contains a tomb

multiples
numbers that can be divided by another number with nothing left over

smog
polluted fog

three-dimensional
having height, width, and depth

trust
a fund established to provide annual income

wedges
triangular pieces that are pounded between two objects to split them

ONLINE RESOURCES

To learn more about the Taj Mahal, visit our free resource websites below.

Visit **abdocorelibrary.com** for free Common Core resources for teachers and students, including vetted activities, multimedia, and booklinks, for deeper subject comprehension.

Visit **abdobooklinks.com** for free additional online weblinks for further learning. These links are routinely monitored and updated to provide the most current information available.

LEARN MORE

Buckley, A. M. *India*. Minneapolis, MN: Abdo, 2012.

Jackson, Tom. *Wonders of the World*. New York: DK, 2014.

INDEX

Agra, 5, 8, 11, 15, 27, 30

balance, 8, 18, 20, 29
bilateral symmetry, 18

commercial development, 35

domes, 16, 22, 28–29, 34

foundation, 25–26, 39, 41

geometry, 18, 29
grid system, 18

hierarchy, 22

Karim, Mir Abd-ul, 15
Khan, Makramat, 15

Lahauri, Ustad Ahmad, 15

maintenance, 34, 35, 39
marble, 8, 18, 22, 26, 27, 28, 33, 34, 39
mausoleum, 5, 6–7, 8, 10, 18, 20, 21, 22, 25, 28, 30, 34
Mecca, 30
minaret, 5, 20, 31, 39
mosque, 8, 18, 20
Mughal empire, 10–11, 12, 16, 28, 34
Mumtaz Mahal, 7, 8, 12–13, 16, 22, 29–30

parallax, 20
pollution, 34–35, 39

sandstone, 8, 26, 27
Shah Jahan, 7, 12–13, 15, 18, 22, 26, 30
Singh, Raja Jai, 23
surface treatment, 39
symbolism, 20–22

tourism, 33, 35
trust, 30

workers, 25–28

Yamuna River, 5, 16, 34, 39

About the Author

Laura K. Murray has written more than 40 nonfiction books for children. She lives in Minnesota and enjoys learning about places around the world.